THE BACH FAKE BOOK

Index by BWV Number
Page 124

Cherry Lane Music Company
Director of Publications/Project Editor: Mark Phillips
Project Coordinator: Rebecca Skidmore

Cherry Lane gratefully acknowledges David Pearl for his help in the preparation of this book.

ISBN 978-1-60378-179-4

Visit our website at www.cherrylaneprint.com

CONTENTS

AIR ON THE G STRING, BWV 1068
from Orchestral Suite No. 3 in D major

Johann Sebastian Bach

ARIA, BWV 988
from the Goldberg Variations

Johann Sebastian Bach

ARIOSO, BWV 156
from Cantata 156

Johann Sebastian Bach

BIST DU BEI MIR, BWV 508
from the Anna Magdalena Notebook

Johann Sebastian Bach
(attributed to G.H. Stözel)

BRANDENBURG CONCERTO NO. 1 IN F, BWV 1046

First Movement

Johann Sebastian Bach

BRANDENBURG CONCERTO NO. 1 IN F, BWV 1046
Minuet

Johann Sebastian Bach

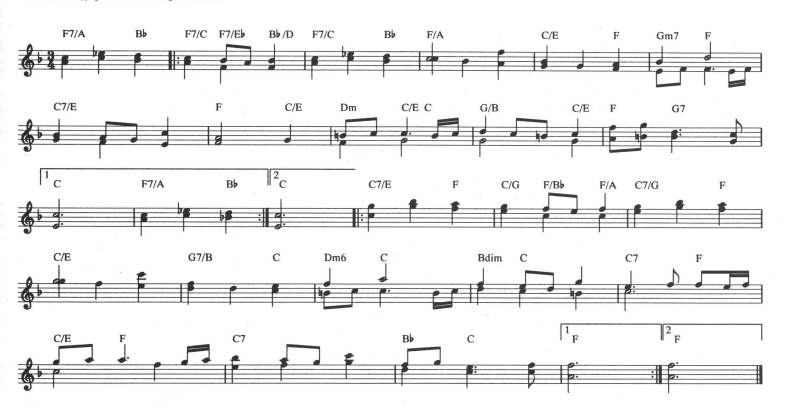

BRANDENBURG CONCERTO NO. 1 IN F, BWV 1046
Polacca

Johann Sebastian Bach

BRANDENBURG CONCERTO NO. 1 IN F, BWV 1046
Second Movement

Johann Sebastian Bach

BRANDENBURG CONCERTO NO. 1 IN F, BWV 1046
Third Movement

Johann Sebastian Bach

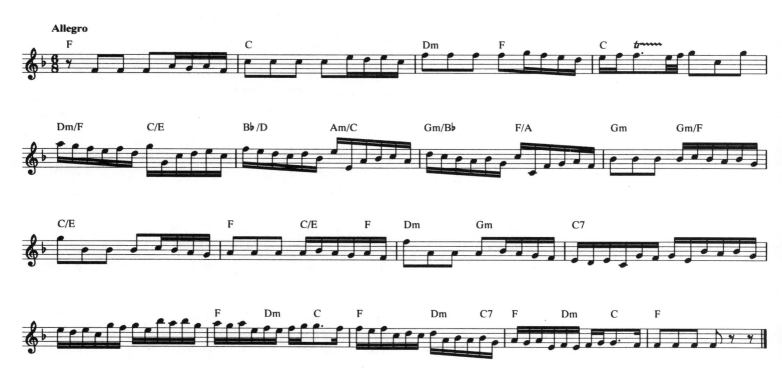

BRANDENBURG CONCERTO NO. 2 IN F, BWV 1047
First Movement

Johann Sebastian Bach

BRANDENBURG CONCERTO NO. 2 IN F, BWV 1047
Second Movement

Johann Sebastian Bach

BRANDENBURG CONCERTO NO. 2 IN F, BWV 1047
Third Movement

Johann Sebastian Bach

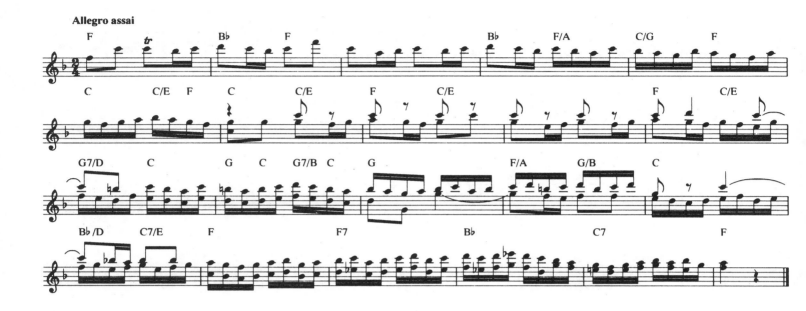

BRANDENBURG CONCERTO NO. 3 IN G, BWV 1048
First Movement

Johann Sebastian Bach

BRANDENBURG CONCERTO NO. 3 IN G, BWV 1048
Third Movement

Johann Sebastian Bach

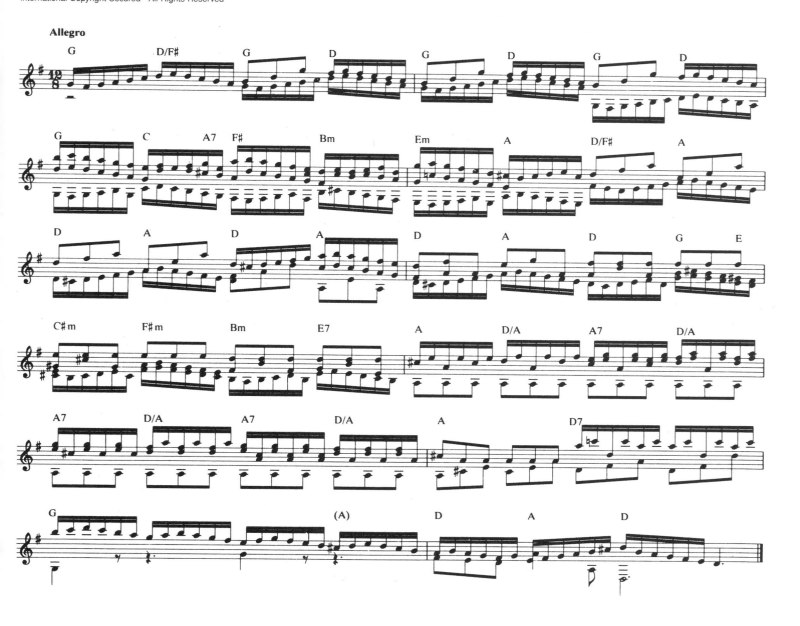

BRANDENBURG CONCERTO NO. 4 IN G, BWV 1049
First Movement

Johann Sebastian Bach

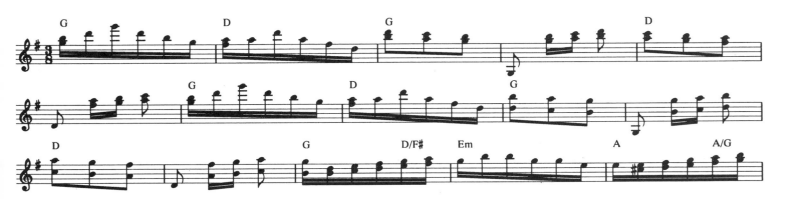

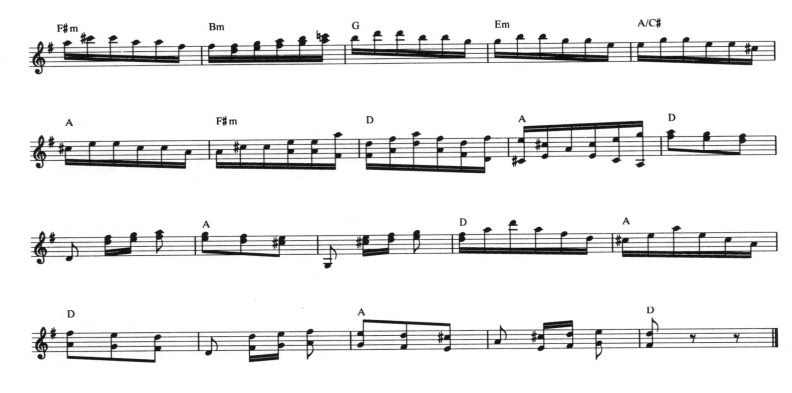

BRANDENBURG CONCERTO NO. 4 IN G, BWV 1049
Third Movement

Johann Sebastian Bach

BRANDENBURG CONCERTO NO. 5 IN D, BWV 1050
First Movement

Johann Sebastian Bach

BRANDENBURG CONCERTO NO. 5 IN D, BWV 1050
Second Movement

Johann Sebastian Bach

BRANDENBURG CONCERTO NO. 5 IN D, BWV 1050
Third Movement

Johann Sebastian Bach

BRANDENBURG CONCERTO NO. 6 IN B♭, BWV 1051

First Movement

Johann Sebastian Bach

BRANDENBURG CONCERTO NO. 6 IN B♭, BWV 1051
Third Movement

Johann Sebastian Bach

CANTATA 29, BWV 29
Aria: Gedenk' an uns mit deiner Liebe

Johann Sebastian Bach

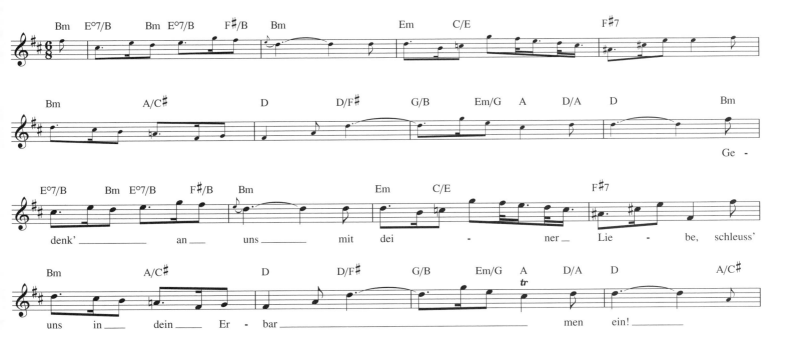

CANTATA 51, BWV 51

Aria: Jauchzet Gott in allen Landen

Johann Sebastian Bach

CANTATA 78, BWV 78

Chorale: Herr, Ich glaube, hilf mir Schwachen

Johann Sebastian Bach

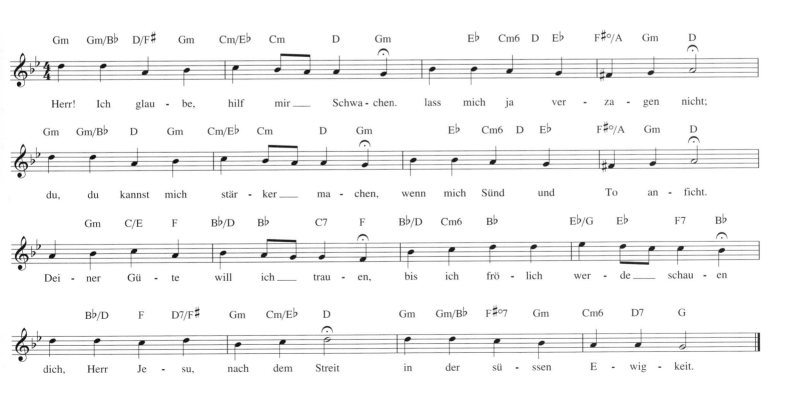

CANTATA 82, BWV 82
Aria: Ich habe genug

Johann Sebastian Bach

CANTATA 143, BWV 143
Chorale: Du Friedefürst, Herr Jesu Christ

Johann Sebastian Bach

CANTATA 156, BWV 156
Sinfonia

Johann Sebastian Bach

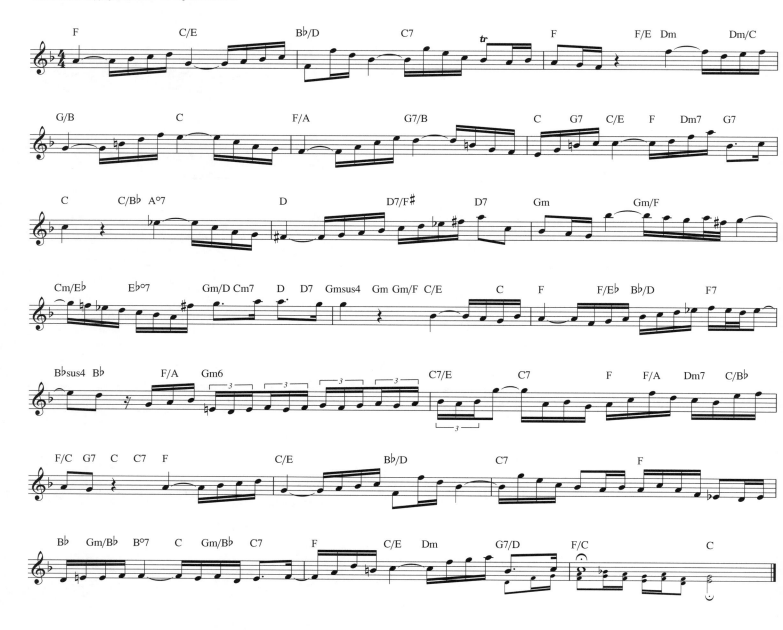

CANTATA 199, BWV 199
Aria: Tief gebückt und voller Reue

Johann Sebastian Bach

Gott, vor Dir. Tief ge-bückt un vol-ler Reu-e,
und vol-ler Reu-
e, tief ge-bückt und vol-ler
Reu-e lieg ich, lieg ich lieb-ster Gott vor Dir.
Tief ge-bückt, tief ge-bückt und vol-ler Rue-e lieg
ich, lieb-ster Gott, lieg ich, lieb-ster Gott, vor Dir.

CANTATA 202 (WEDDING CANTATA), BWV 202
Aria: Sich üben im lieben

Johann Sebastian Bach

Sich ü-ben_ im
lie-ben, in Scher-zen_ sich her-zen ist be-ser_ als Flo-rens_ ver-gäng-li-che_ Lust, sich

ü - ben — im lie - ben, in Scher - zen — sich her - zen ist bes - ser als Flo - rens — ver -

gäng - li - che Lust, sich ü - ben — im lie - ben, in Scher - zen — sich her - zen ist bes - ser — als

Flo - rens ver - gäng - li - che — Lust.

Sich ü - ben — im lie - ben, in

Scher - zen — sich her - zen ist bes - ser als Flo - rens ver - gäng - li - che Lust, sich ü - ben — im

D.C. al Fine

lie - ben, in Scher - zen — sich her - zen ist bes - ser als — Flo - rens — ver - gäng - li - che Lust.

CANTATA 202 (WEDDING CANTATA), BWV 202
Aria: Wenn die Frühlingslüfte streichen

Johann Sebastian Bach

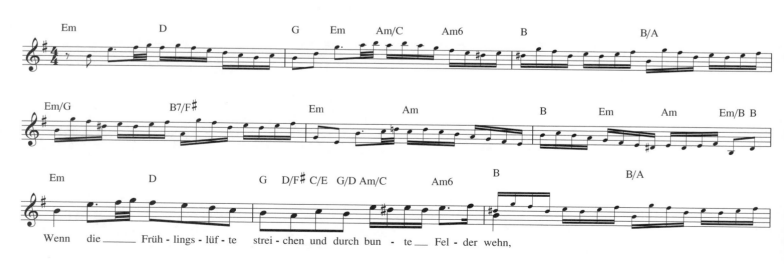

Wenn die _____ Früh - lings - lüf - te strei - chen und durch bun - te ___ Fel - der wehn,

26

CANTATA 202 (WEDDING CANTATA), BWV 202
Gavotte

Johann Sebastian Bach

CANTATA 211 (COFFEE CANTATA), BWV 211
Aria: Ei! Wie schmeckt der Coffee süsse

Johann Sebastian Bach

CANTATA 212 (PEASANT CANTATA), BWV 212

Aria: Dein Wachsthum sie feste

Johann Sebastian Bach

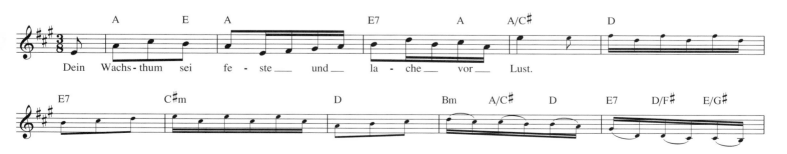

CANTATA 212 (PEASANT CANTATA), BWV 212

Chorus: Wir gehn nun, wo der Tudelsack

Johann Sebastian Bach

CELLO AND CONTINUO SONATA NO. 3, BWV 1029
Second Movement

Johann Sebastian Bach

CELLO SUITE NO. 1 IN G MAJOR, BWV 1007
Prelude

Johann Sebastian Bach

Briskly

CELLO SUITE NO. 2 IN D MINOR, BWV 1008
Menuet

Johann Sebastian Bach

CELLO SUITE NO. 3 IN C MAJOR, BWV 1009
Bourrée I

Johann Sebastian Bach

CELLO SUITE NO. 3 IN C MAJOR, BWV 1009
Bourrée II

Johann Sebastian Bach

Bourrée I D.C.
(no repeats)

CELLO SUITE NO. 4 IN E♭ MAJOR, BWV 1010
Bourrée I

Johann Sebastian Bach

CELLO SUITE NO. 4 IN E♭ MAJOR, BWV 1010
Bourrée II

Johann Sebastian Bach

CELLO SUITE NO. 6 IN D MAJOR, BWV 1012

Gavottes I & II

Johann Sebastian Bach

CHORALE PRELUDE FOR ORGAN, BWV 722
Gelobet sei'st du, Jesu Christ

Johann Sebastian Bach

CHORALE PRELUDE FOR ORGAN, BWV 650
Kommst du nun, Jesus

Johann Sebastian Bach

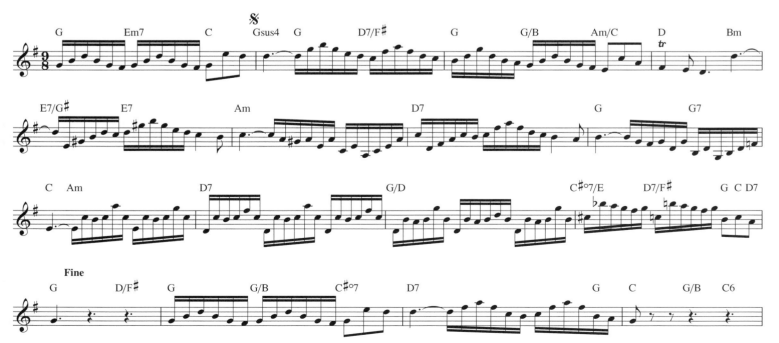

CHORALE PRELUDE FOR ORGAN, BWV 731
Liebster Jesu, wir sind hier

Johann Sebastian Bach

CHORALE PRELUDE FOR ORGAN, BWV 659
Nun komm' der Heiden Heiland

Johann Sebastian Bach

CHRISTMAS ORATORIO, BWV 248
Aria: Bereite dich, Zion

Johann Sebastian Bach

CHRISTMAS ORATORIO, BWV 248

Aria: Ich will nur dir zu Ehren leben

Johann Sebastian Bach

CHRISTMAS ORATORIO, BWV 248
Choral: Brich an, a schönes Morgenlicht

Johann Sebastian Bach

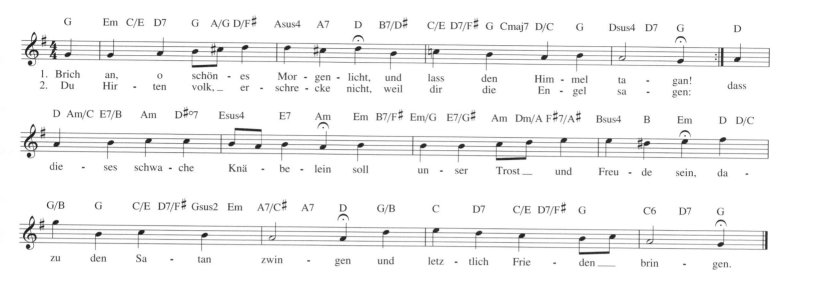

1. Brich an, o schön - es Mor - gen - licht, und lass den Him - mel ta - gan!
2. Du Hir - ten volk, er - schre - cke nicht, weil dir die En - gel sa - gen: dass

die - ses schwa - che Knä - be - lein soll un - ser Trost und Freu - de sein, da -

zu den Sa - tan zwin - gen und letz - tlich Frie - den brin - gen.

CHRISTMAS ORATORIO, BWV 248
Chorus: Jauchzet, frohlocket

Johann Sebastian Bach

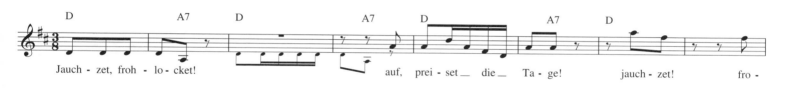

Jauch - zet, froh - lo - cket! auf, prei - set die Ta - ge! jauch - zet! fro -

lo - cket! jauch - zet, froh - lo - cket, auf, prei - set die Ta - ge,

rüh - met, was heu - te der Höch - ste ge - than!

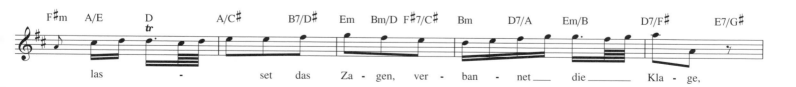

las - set das Za - gen, ver - ban - net die Kla - ge,

las - set das Za - gen, ver - ban - net die Kla - ge, ver - ban - net die

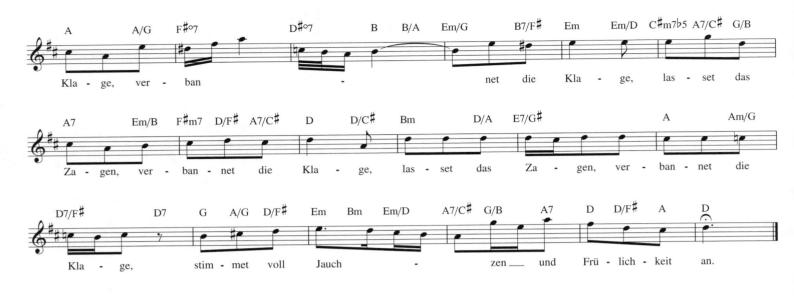

Kla - ge, ver - ban - net die Kla - ge, las - set das

Za - gen, ver - ban - net die Kla - ge, las - set das Za - gen, ver - ban - net die

Kla - ge, stim - met voll Jauch - zen und Frü - lich - keit an.

CHRISTMAS ORATORIO, BWV 248
Sinfonia

Johann Sebastian Bach

COME, SWEET DEATH, BWV 478
(Komm, süsser Tod) Hymn from the Schemelli Songbook

Johann Sebastian Bach

Komm, sü - sser _____ Tod, komm, sel' - ge _____ Ruh'!
Komm, sü - sser _____ Tod, komm, sel' - ge _____ Ruh'!

Komm, und füh - re mich _____ in Frie - de, weil ich der
Ich will nun Je - sum se - hen und bei den

Welt _____ bin _____ mü - de. Ach, komm, ich wart' auf
En - gel _____ ste - hen. Es ist ja nun voll -

dich, komm _____ bald und füh - re mich,
bracht, Welt, _____ da - rum gu - te Nacht,

drück' mir _____ die _____ Au - gen _____ zu. Komm, _____ sel' - ge Ruh'!
mein' Au - gen _____ schliess' _____ ich _____ zu. Komm, _____ sel' - ge Ruh'!

CONCERTO FOR THREE KEYBOARDS NO. 1 IN D MINOR, BWV 1063
Second Movement

Johann Sebastian Bach

Alla Siciliana

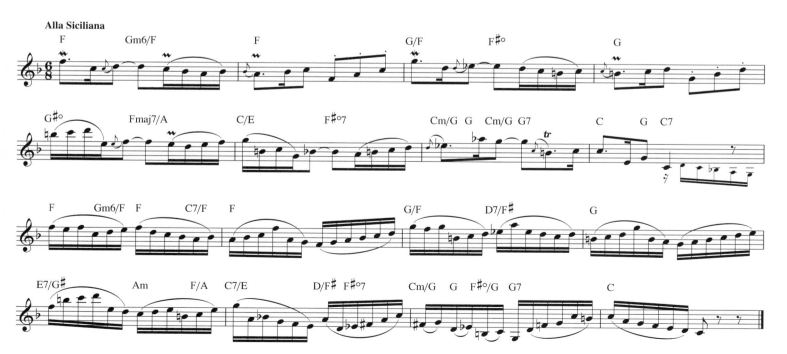

CONCERTO FOR TWO KEYBOARDS NO. 1 IN C MINOR, BWV 1060
Second Movement

Johann Sebastian Bach

CONCERTO FOR TWO VIOLINS IN D MINOR, BWV 1043
Second Movement

Johann Sebastian Bach

DER LIEBEN SONNE LICHT UND PRACHT, BWV 446
Aria from the Schemelli Songbook

Johann Sebastian Bach

Der lie-ben Son-ne Licht und — Pracht hat nun den Tag voll-füh-ret, die Welt hat sich zur

Ruh' ge-macht: thu, Seel', was dir ge-büh-ret, trirr an die Him-mels-thür' und

sing' ein Lied da-für, lass dei-ne Oh-ren, — Herz und Sinn auf Je-sum sein ge-rich-tet — hin!

DIR, DIR, JEHOVAH, WILL ICH SINGEN, BWV 452
Aria from the Schemelli Songbook

Johann Sebastian Bach

Dir, dir, — Je-ho-vah, will — ich sin-gen, denn wo ist
Dir will — ich — mei-ne Lie-der brin-gen, ach, gib mir

wohl ein — sol-cher — Gott wie du? } dass ich — es thu' im — Na-
dei-nes — Gei-stes Kraft da-zu, }

men Je-su Christ, so wie es — dir durch ihn — ge-fäl-lig — ist.

ENGLISH SUITE NO. 2 IN A MINOR, BWV 807
Gigue

Johann Sebastian Bach

Presto

ENGLISH SUITE NO. 2 IN A MINOR, BWV 807
Sarabande

Johann Sebastian Bach

ENGLISH SUITE NO. 3 IN G MINOR, BWV 808
Gavotte I

Johann Sebastian Bach

ENGLISH SUITE NO. 5 IN E MAJOR, BWV 810
Passepied I

Johann Sebastian Bach

ENGLISH SUITE NO. 5 IN E MAJOR, BWV 810
Passepied II

Johann Sebastian Bach

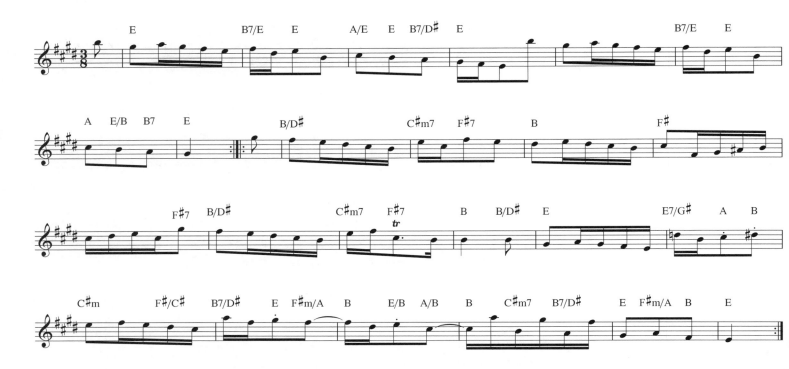

FANTASIA FOR ORGAN IN G MAJOR, BWV 572

Johann Sebastian Bach

51

FANTASIA IN G MINOR, BWV 542

Johann Sebastian Bach

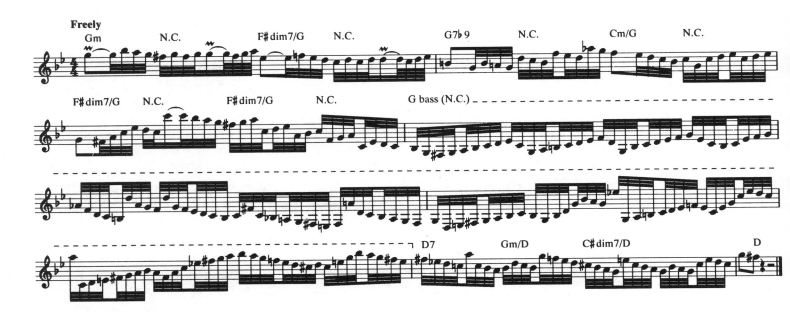

FLUTE AND CONTINUO SONATA NO. 1, BWV 1033
First Movement

Johann Sebastian Bach

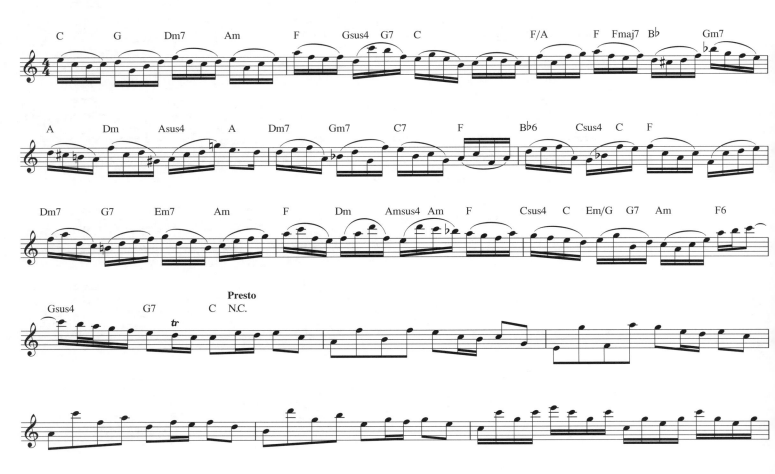

FLUTE AND CONTINUO SONATA NO. 1, BWV 1033
Minuets I & II

Johann Sebastian Bach

FLUTE AND CONTINUO SONATA NO. 2, BWV 1034
Third Movement

Johann Sebastian Bach

FLUTE AND HARPSICHORD SONATA NO. 2, BWV 1031
Siciliano

Johann Sebastian Bach

FRENCH SUITE NO. 1 IN D MINOR, BWV 812
Minuet II

Johann Sebastian Bach

FRENCH SUITE NO. 3 IN B MINOR, BWV 814
Sarabande

Johann Sebastian Bach

FRENCH SUITE NO. 4 IN E♭ MAJOR, BWV 815
Sarabande

Johann Sebastian Bach

FRENCH SUITE NO. 5 IN G MAJOR, BWV 816
Allemande

Johann Sebastian Bach

FRENCH SUITE NO. 5 IN G MAJOR, BWV 816
Gavotte

Johann Sebastian Bach

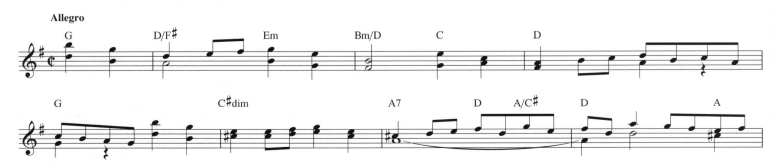

FRENCH SUITE NO. 5 IN G MAJOR, BWV 816
Sarabande

Johann Sebastian Bach

Andante cantabile

FUGUE IN C MINOR, BWV 847
from The Well Tempered Clavier Book I

Johann Sebastian Bach

ITALIAN CONCERTO, BWV 971
First Movement

Johann Sebastian Bach

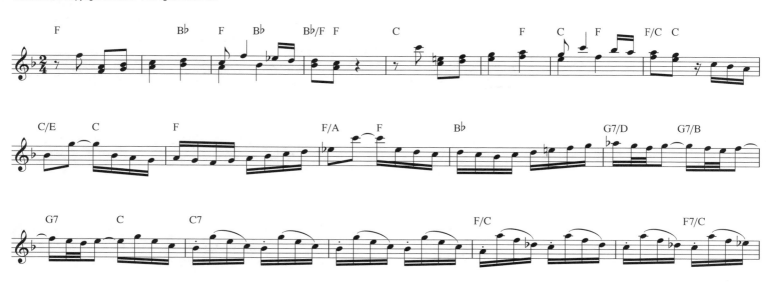

ITALIAN CONCERTO, BWV 971
Second Movement

Johann Sebastian Bach

ITALIAN CONCERTO, BWV 971
Third Movement

Johann Sebastian Bach

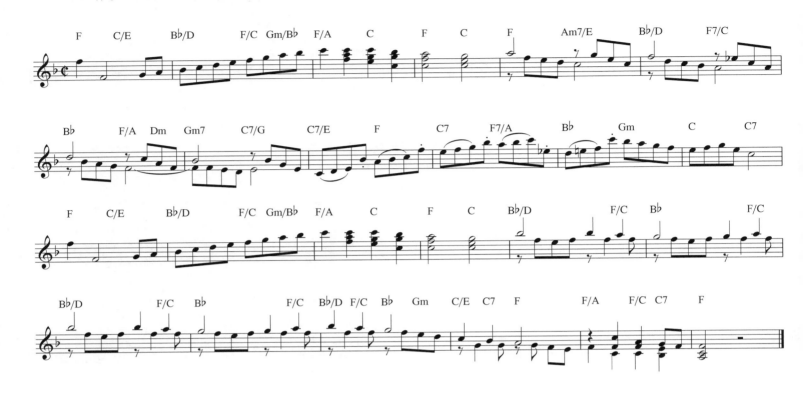

JESU, JOY OF MAN'S DESIRING, BWV 147
from Cantata 147

Johann Sebastian Bach

KEEP, O MY SPIRIT, BWV 248
Aria from Christmas Oratorio

Johann Sebastian Bach

KEYBOARD CONCERTO NO. 1 IN D MINOR, BWV 1052
First Movement

Johann Sebastian Bach

KEYBOARD CONCERTO NO. 1 IN D MINOR, BWV 1052
Second Movement

Johann Sebastian Bach

KEYBOARD CONCERTO NO. 1 IN D MINOR, BWV 1052
Third Movement

Johann Sebastian Bach

KEYBOARD CONCERTO NO. 2 IN E MAJOR, BWV 1053
First Movement

Johann Sebastian Bach

KEYBOARD CONCERTO NO. 2 IN E MAJOR, BWV 1053
Second Movement

Johann Sebastian Bach

KEYBOARD CONCERTO NO. 2 IN E MAJOR, BWV 1053
Third Movement

Johann Sebastian Bach

KEYBOARD CONCERTO NO. 5 IN F MINOR, BWV 1056
Second Movement

Johann Sebastian Bach

KEYBOARD PARTITA NO. 1 IN B♭ MAJOR, BWV 825
Minuet

Johann Sebastian Bach

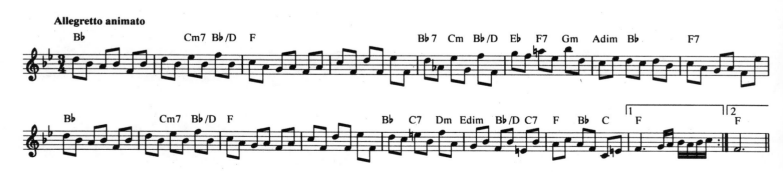

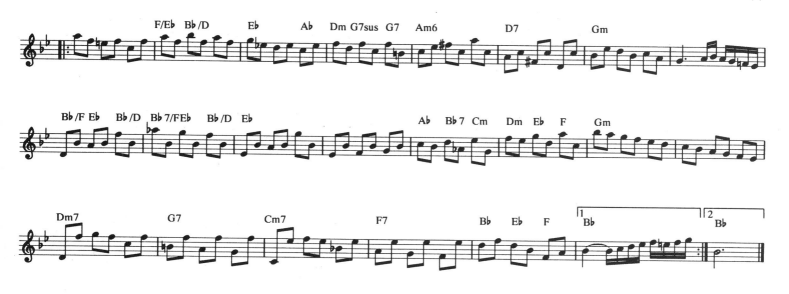

KEYBOARD PARTITA NO. 3 IN A MINOR, BWV 827

Scherzo

Johann Sebastian Bach

KEYBOARD PARTITA NO. 4 IN D MAJOR, BWV 828

Aria

Johann Sebastian Bach

LITTLE FUGUE IN G MINOR, BWV 578
Fugue Theme

Johann Sebastian Bach

LUTE SUITE IN E MAJOR, BWV 1006a
Gigue

Johann Sebastian Bach

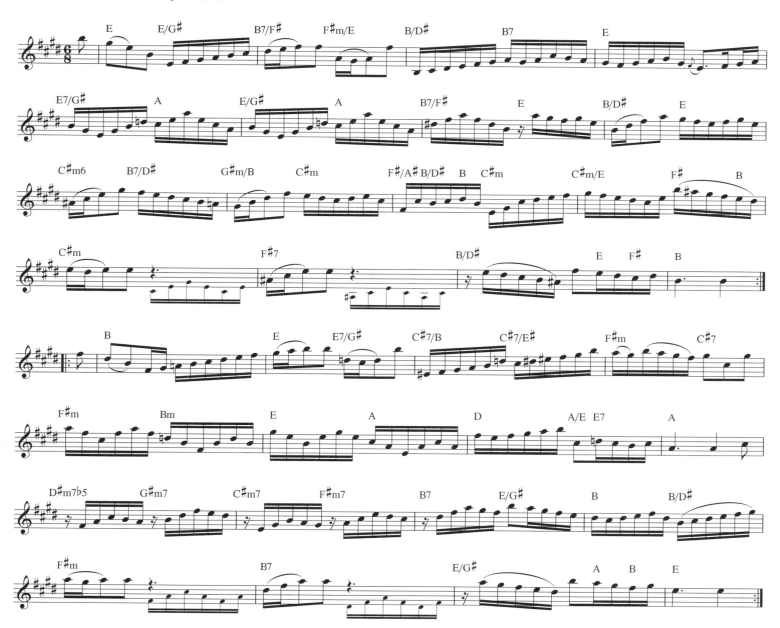

LUTE SUITE IN E MAJOR, BWV 1006a
Minuet I

Johann Sebastian Bach

LUTE SUITE IN E MAJOR, BWV 1006a
Minuet II

Johann Sebastian Bach

LUTE SUITE IN E MINOR, BWV 996
Bourrée

Johann Sebastian Bach

LUTE SUITE IN G MINOR, BWV 995
Courante

Johann Sebastian Bach

LUTE SUITE IN G MINOR, BWV 995
Gavotte I

Johann Sebastian Bach

LUTE SUITE IN G MINOR, BWV 995
Gavotte II en Rondeau

Johann Sebastian Bach

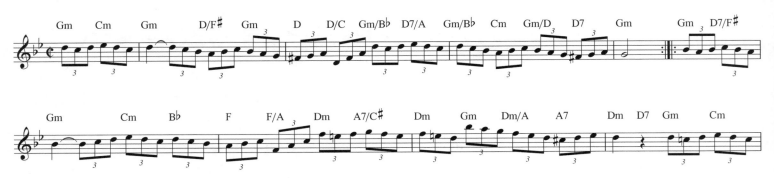

LUTE SUITE IN G MINOR, BWV 995
Prelude

Johann Sebastian Bach

MAGNIFICAT, BWV 243

Aria: Et exsultavit

Johann Sebastian Bach

MAGNIFICAT, BWV 243
Aria: Et misericordia

Johann Sebastian Bach

MAGNIFICAT, BWV 243
Aria: Quia respexit humilitatem

Johann Sebastian Bach

MAGNIFICAT, BWV 243
Coro (Opening Theme)

Johann Sebastian Bach

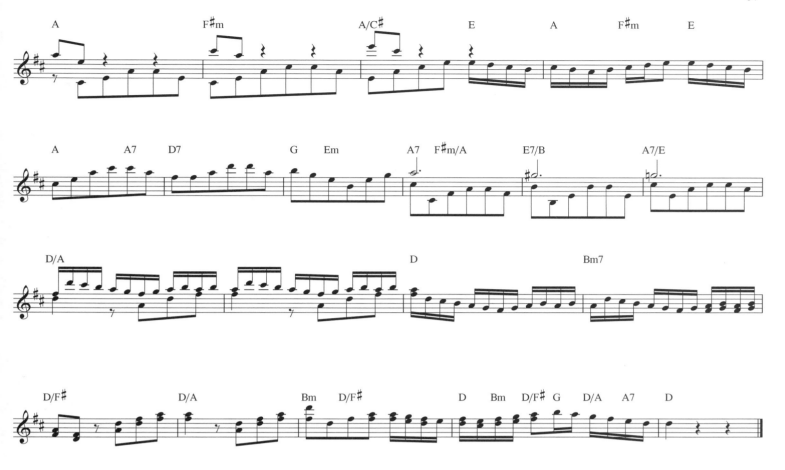

MARCH IN D MAJOR, BWV Anh. 122
from the Anna Magdalena Notebook

Johann Sebastian Bach

MASS IN B MINOR, BWV 232
Agnus Dei

Johann Sebastian Bach

MASS IN B MINOR, BWV 232
Et resurrexit

Johann Sebastian Bach

MASS IN B MINOR, BWV 232
Gloria

Johann Sebastian Bach

MINUET I IN G MAJOR, BWV Anh. 114

from the Anna Magdalena Notebook

Johann Sebastian Bach

MINUET IN G MAJOR, BWV Anh. 116

from the Anna Magdalena Notebook

Johann Sebastian Bach

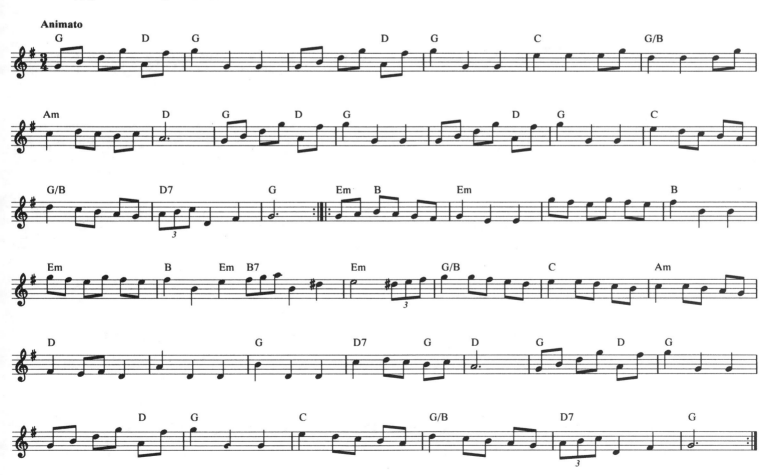

MUSETTE IN D MAJOR, BWV Anh. 126
from the Anna Magdalena Notebook

Johann Sebastian Bach

MY HEART EVER FAITHFUL, BWV 68
Aria from Cantata 68

Johann Sebastian Bach

A - way_ with com- plain- ing, a - way_ with com- plain - ing, Faith ev - er main- tain - ing, My

Je - sus is here! My heart_ ev- er faith- ful, Sing prais- es, be joy - ful, My

heart_ ev- er faith- ful, Sing prais- es, be joy - ful, sing prais- es, be joy - ful, Thy Je - sus is here, Sing prais- es, be

joy- ful, sing prais - es, be joy - ful, My heart_ ev- er faith- ful, Sing prais - es, be joy - ful, sing

prais- es, be joy - ful, Thy_ Je - sus is here!

O JESULEIN SÜSS, BWV 493
Hymn from the Schemelli Songbook

Johann Sebastian Bach

O Je - su - lein süss, o Je - su - lein mild, dein's
O Je - su - lein süss, o Je - su - lein mild, dein's
O Je - su - lein süss, o Je - su - lein mild, mit

Va - ters Will'n hast du _____ er - füllt, bist
Va - ters Zorn hast du _____ ge - stillt, du
Freud' hast du die Welt _____ er - füllt, du

kom - men aus dem Him - mel - reich, uns
zahlst für uns all un - sre Schuld und
kommst her - ab vom Him - mels - saal zu

ar - men Men - schen wor - den gleich, o
bringst uns in dein's Va - ters Huld, o
trö - sten uns im Jam - mer - tal, o

Je - su - lein süss, o Je - su - lein mild!
Je - su - lein süss, o Je - su - lein mild!
Je - su - lein süss, o Je - su - lein mild!

OBOE D'AMORE CONCERTO IN D MINOR, BWV 1059

First Movement

Johann Sebastian Bach

OBOE D'AMORE CONCERTO IN D MINOR, BWV 1059
Third Movement

Johann Sebastian Bach

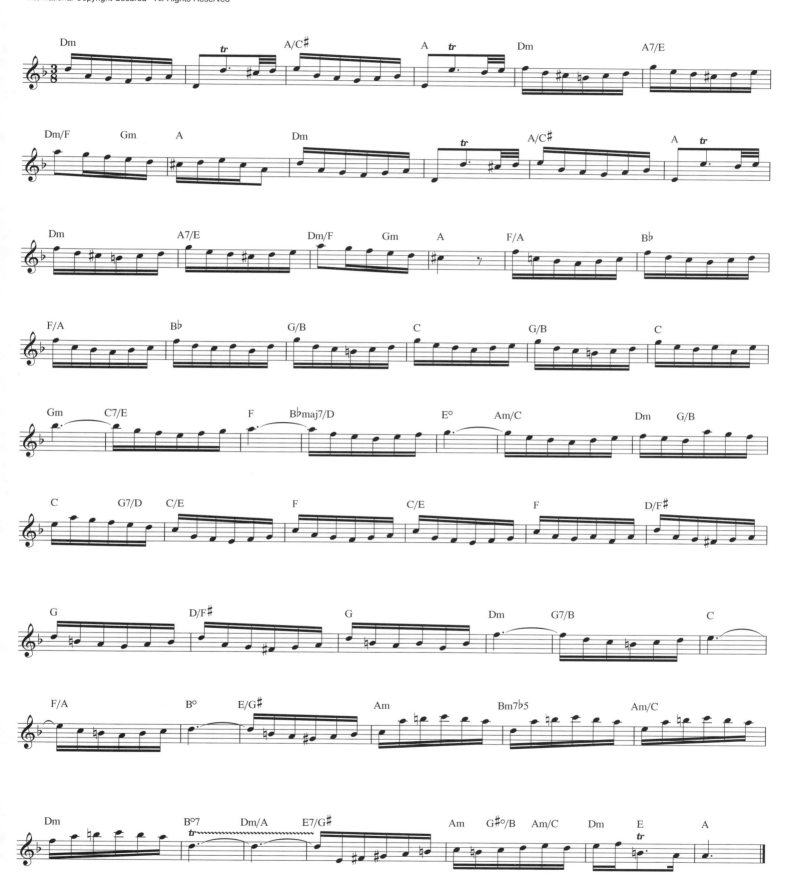

ORCHESTRAL SUITE NO. 1, BWV 1066

Gavotte I

Johann Sebastian Bach

ORCHESTRAL SUITE NO. 1, BWV 1066

Passepied I

Johann Sebastian Bach

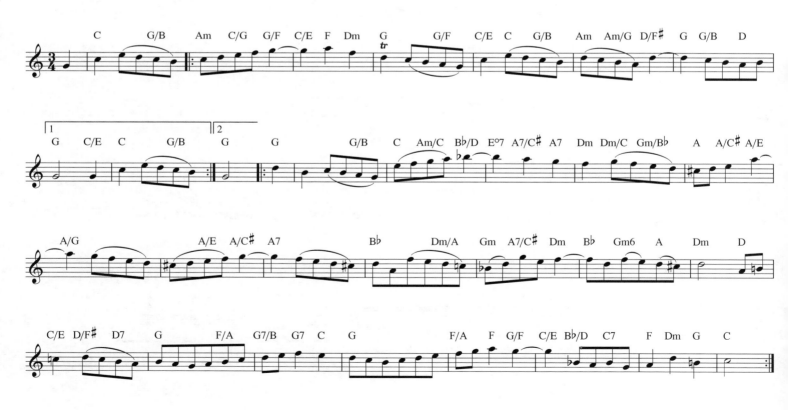

ORCHESTRAL SUITE NO. 2 IN B MINOR, BWV 1067
Badinerie

Johann Sebastian Bach

ORCHESTRAL SUITE NO. 2 IN B MINOR, BWV 1067
Polonaise

Johann Sebastian Bach

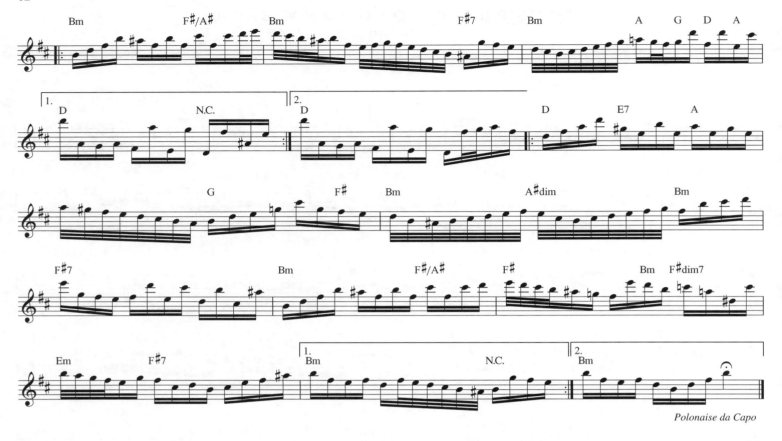

ORCHESTRAL SUITE NO. 2, BWV 1067
Rondeau

Johann Sebastian Bach

PASSACAGLIA FOR ORGAN IN C MINOR, BWV 582

Johann Sebastian Bach

PASTORALE FOR ORGAN IN F MAJOR, BWV 590
First Movement

Johann Sebastian Bach

PASTORALE FOR ORGAN IN F MAJOR, BWV 590
Third Movement

Johann Sebastian Bach

PRELUDE FOR LUTE IN C MINOR, BWV 999

Johann Sebastian Bach

SHEEP MAY SAFELY GRAZE, BWV 208
Aria from Cantata 208

Johann Sebastian Bach

SLEEPERS, AWAKE, BWV 140
(Wachet auf!) from Cantata 140

Johann Sebastian Bach

ST. JOHN PASSION, BWV 245
Aria: Von den Stricken meiner Sünden

Johann Sebastian Bach

ST. JOHN PASSION, BWV 245
Chorale: O grosse Lieb', o Lieb'

Johann Sebastian Bach

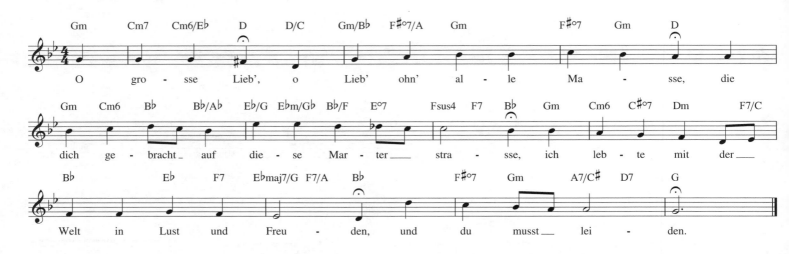

ST. MATTHEW PASSION, BWV 244
Choral: Ich will hier bei dir stehen

Johann Sebastian Bach

ST. MATTHEW PASSION, BWV 244
Choral: O Haupt voll Blut und Wunden

Johann Sebastian Bach

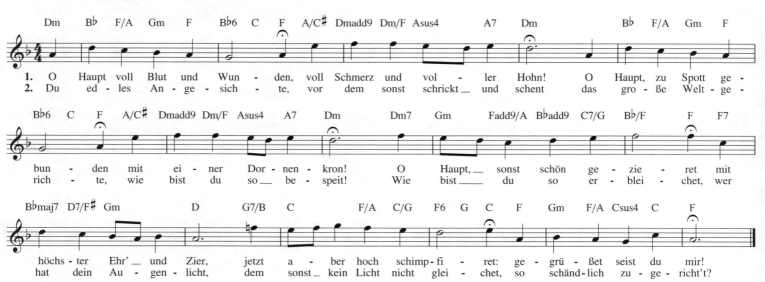

ST. MATTHEW PASSION, BWV 244

Chorus: Wir setzen uns mit Tränen nieder

Johann Sebastian Bach

TOCCATA AND FUGUE IN D MINOR, BWV 565

Johann Sebastian Bach

104

TWO-PART INVENTION IN A MINOR, BWV 784

Johann Sebastian Bach

TWO-PART INVENTION IN C MAJOR, BWV 772

Johann Sebastian Bach

TWO-PART INVENTION IN D MINOR, BWV 775

Johann Sebastian Bach

VERGISS MEIN NICHT, BWV 505

Aria from the Schemelli Songbook

Johann Sebastian Bach

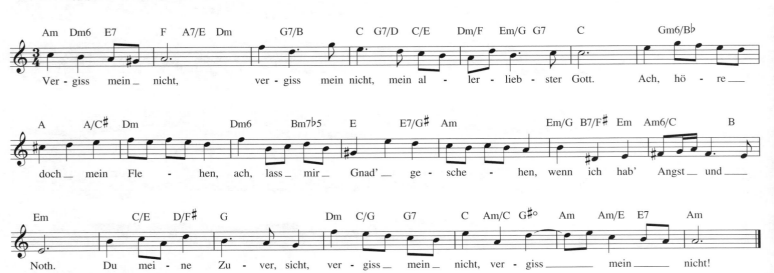

VIOLIN AND CONTINUO SONATA IN E MINOR, BWV 1023
Allemande

Johann Sebastian Bach

VIOLIN AND CONTINUO SONATA IN E MINOR, BWV 1023
Gigue

Johann Sebastian Bach

109

VIOLIN AND KEYBOARD SONATA NO. 4 IN C MINOR, BWV 1017
Fourth Movement

This Arrangement Copyright © 2010 Cherry Lane Music Company
International Copyright Secured All Rights Reserved

Johann Sebastian Bach

VIOLIN AND KEYBOARD SONATA NO. 4 IN C MINOR, BWV 1017
Siciliano

Johann Sebastian Bach

VIOLIN AND KEYBOARD SONATA NO. 6 IN G MAJOR, BWV 1019
Cembalo Solo

Johann Sebastian Bach

VIOLIN CONCERTO IN A MINOR, BWV 1041
First Movement

Johann Sebastian Bach

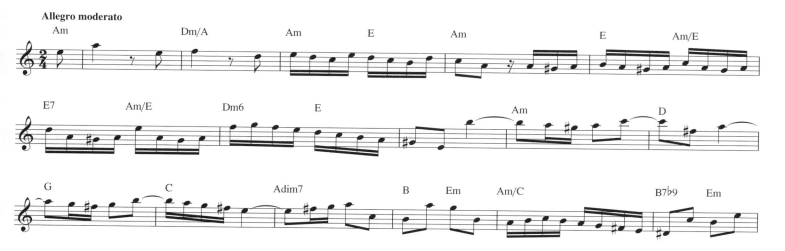

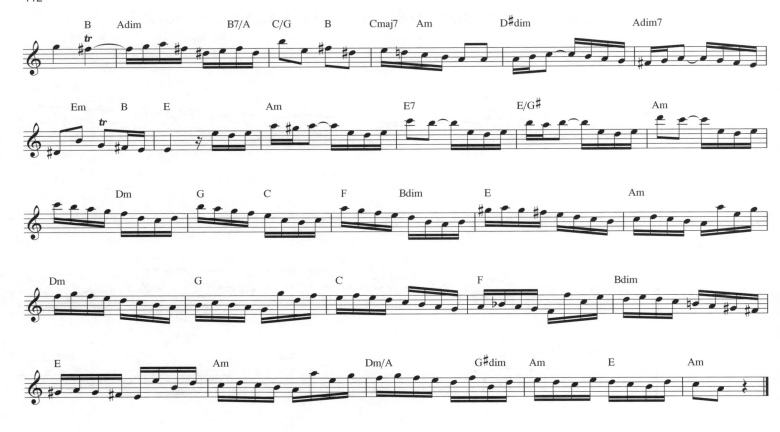

VIOLIN CONCERTO IN A MINOR, BWV 1041
Second Movement

Johann Sebastian Bach

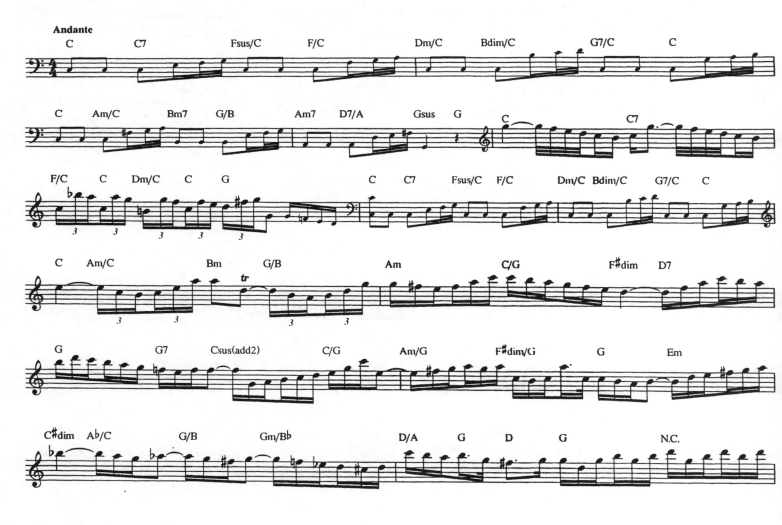

VIOLIN CONCERTO NO. 2 IN E MAJOR, BWV 1042
First Movement

Johann Sebastian Bach

VIOLIN PARTITA NO. 1 IN B MINOR, BWV 1002
Bourrée

Johann Sebastian Bach

VIOLIN PARTITA NO. 1 IN B MINOR, BWV 1002
Sarabande

Johann Sebastian Bach

VIOLIN PARTITA NO. 2 IN D MINOR, BWV 1004
Chaconne

Johann Sebastian Bach

VIOLIN PARTITA NO. 3 IN E MAJOR, BWV 1006
Gavotte en Rondeau

Johann Sebastian Bach

VIOLIN PARTITA NO. 3 IN E MAJOR, BWV 1006
Prelude

Johann Sebastian Bach

VIOLIN SONATA NO. 1 IN G MINOR, BWV 1001
Presto

Johann Sebastian Bach

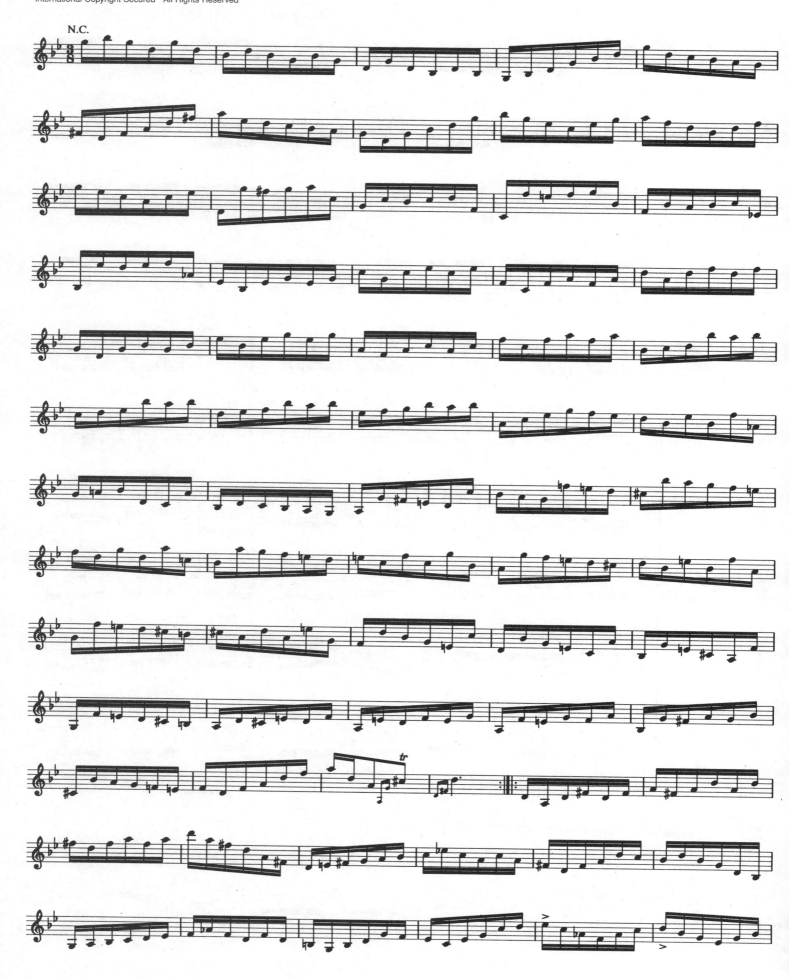

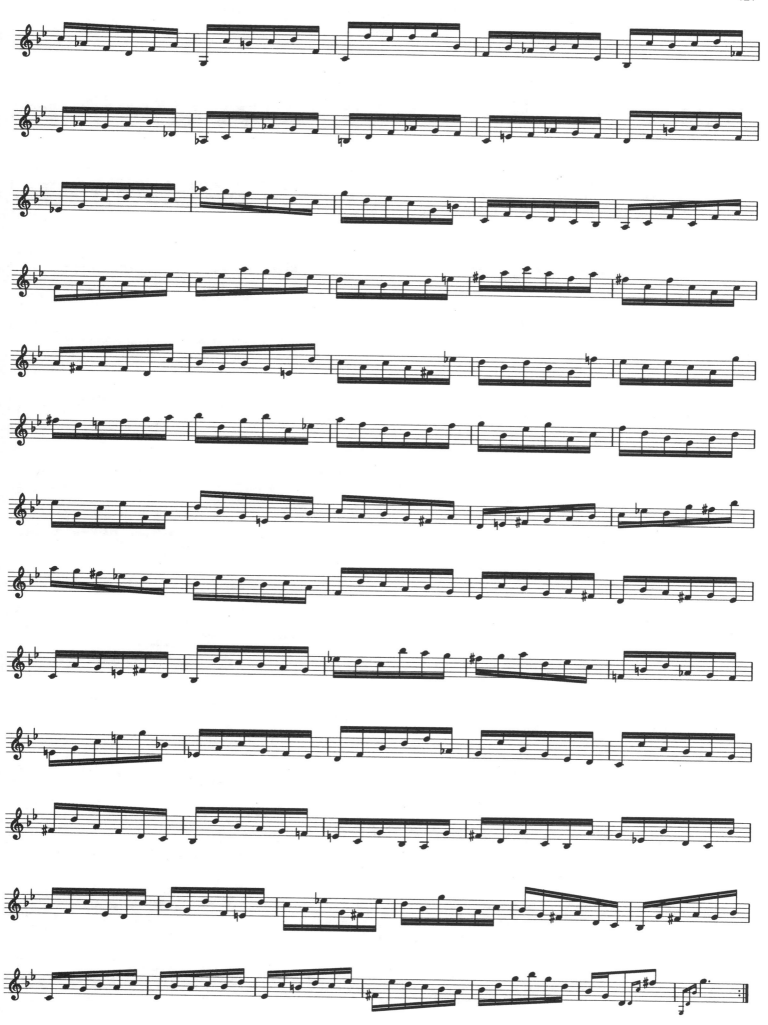

VIOLIN SONATA NO. 3 IN C MAJOR, BWV 1005

Allegro

Johann Sebastian Bach

INDEX BY BWV NUMBER

great songs series

This legendary series has delighted players and performers for generations.

Great Songs of the Fifties

Features rock, pop, country, Broadway and movie tunes, including: All Shook Up • At the Hop • Blue Suede Shoes • Dream Lover • Fly Me to the Moon • Kansas City • Love Me Tender • Misty • Peggy Sue • Rock Around the Clock • Sea of Love • Sixteen Tons • Take the "A" Train • Wonderful! Wonderful! • and more. Includes an introduction by award-winning journalist Bruce Pollock.
02500323 P/V/G...$16.95

Great Songs of the Sixties, Vol. 1 – Revised

The updated version of this classic book includes 80 faves from the 1960s: Angel of the Morning • Bridge over Troubled Water • Cabaret • Different Drum • Do You Believe in Magic • Eve of Destruction • Monday, Monday • Spinning Wheel • Walk on By • and more.
02509902 P/V/G...$19.95

Great Songs of the Sixties, Vol. 2 – Revised

61 more '60s hits: California Dreamin' • Crying • For Once in My Life • Honey • Little Green Apples • MacArthur Park • Me and Bobby McGee • Nowhere Man • Piece of My Heart • Sugar, Sugar • You Made Me So Very Happy • and more.
02509904 P/V/G...$19.95

Great Songs of the Seventies, Vol. 1 – Revised

This super collection of 70 big hits from the '70s includes: After the Love Has Gone • Afternoon Delight • Annie's Song • Band on the Run • Cold as Ice • FM • Imagine • It's Too Late • Layla • Let It Be • Maggie May • Piano Man • Shelter from the Storm • Superstar • Sweet Baby James • Time in a Bottle • The Way We Were • and more.
02509917 P/V/G...$19.95

Great Songs of the Eighties – Revised

This edition features 50 songs in rock, pop & country styles, plus hits from Broadway and the movies! Songs: Almost Paradise • Angel of the Morning • Do You Really Want to Hurt Me • Endless Love • Flashdance...What a Feeling • Guilty • Hungry Eyes • (Just Like) Starting Over • Let Love Rule • Missing You • Patience • Through the Years • Time After Time • Total Eclipse of the Heart • and more.
02502125 P/V/G...$18.95

Great Songs of the Nineties

Includes: Achy Breaky Heart • Beautiful in My Eyes • Believe • Black Hole Sun • Black Velvet • Blaze of Glory • Building a Mystery • Crash into Me • Fields of Gold • From a Distance • Glycerine • Here and Now • Hold My Hand • I'll Make Love to You • Ironic • Linger • My Heart Will Go On • Waterfalls • Wonderwall • and more.
02500040 P/V/G...$16.95

Great Songs of Broadway

This fabulous collection of 60 standards includes: Getting to Know You • Hello, Dolly! • The Impossible Dream • Let Me Entertain You • My Favorite Things • My Husband Makes Movies • Oh, What a Beautiful Mornin' • On My Own • People • Tomorrow • Try to Remember • Unusual Way • What I Did for Love • and dozens more, plus an introductory article.
02500615 P/V/G...$19.95

Great Songs for Children

90 wonderful, singable favorites kids love: Baa Baa Black Sheep • Bingo • The Candy Man • Do-Re-Mi • Eensy Weensy Spider • The Hokey Pokey • Linus and Lucy • Sing • This Old Man • Yellow Submarine • and more, with a touching foreword by Grammy-winning singer/songwriter Tom Chapin.
02501348 P/V/G...$19.99

Great Songs of Classic Rock

Nearly 50 of the greatest songs of the rock era, including: Against the Wind • Cold As Ice • Don't Stop Believin' • Feels like the First Time • I Can See for Miles • Maybe I'm Amazed • Minute by Minute • Money • Nights in White Satin • Only the Lonely • Open Arms • Rikki Don't Lose That Number • Rosanna • We Are the Champions • and more.
02500801 P/V/G...$19.95

Great Songs of Country Music

This volume features 58 country gems, including: Abilene • Afternoon Delight • Amazed • Annie's Song • Blue • Crazy • Elvira • Fly Away • For the Good Times • Friends in Low Places • The Gambler • Hey, Good Lookin' • I Hope You Dance • Thank God I'm a Country Boy • This Kiss • Your Cheatin' Heart • and more.
02500503 P/V/G...$19.95

Great Songs of Folk Music

Nearly 50 of the most popular folk songs of our time, including: Blowin' in the Wind • The House of the Rising Sun • Puff the Magic Dragon • This Land Is Your Land • Time in a Bottle • The Times They Are A-Changin' • The Unicorn • Where Have All the Flowers Gone? • and more.
02500997 P/V/G...$19.95

Great Songs from The Great American Songbook

52 American classics, including: Ain't That a Kick in the Head • As Time Goes By • Come Fly with Me • Georgia on My Mind • I Get a Kick Out of You • I've Got You Under My Skin • The Lady Is a Tramp • Love and Marriage • Mack the Knife • Misty • Over the Rainbow • People • Take the "A" Train • Thanks for the Memory • and more.
02500760 P/V/G...$16.95

Great Songs of the Movies

Nearly 60 of the best songs popularized in the movies, including: Accidentally in Love • Alfie • Almost Paradise • The Rainbow Connection • Somewhere in My Memory • Take My Breath Away (Love Theme) • Three Coins in the Fountain • (I've Had) the Time of My Life • Up Where We Belong • The Way We Were • and more.
02500967 P/V/G...$19.95

Great Songs of the Pop Era

Over 50 hits from the pop era, including: Every Breath You Take • I'm Every Woman • Just the Two of Us • Leaving on a Jet Plane • My Cherie Amour • Raindrops Keep Fallin' on My Head • Time After Time • (I've Had) the Time of My Life • What a Wonderful World • and more.
02500043 Easy Piano...$16.95

Great Songs of 2000-2009

Over 50 of the decade's biggest hits, including: Accidentally in Love • Breathe (2 AM) • Daughters • Hanging by a Moment • The Middle • The Remedy (I Won't Worry) • Smooth • A Thousand Miles • and more.
02500922 P/V/G...$24.99

Great Songs for Weddings

A beautiful collection of 59 pop standards perfect for wedding ceremonies and receptions, including: Always and Forever • Amazed • Beautiful in My Eyes • Can You Feel the Love Tonight • Endless Love • Love of a Lifetime • Open Arms • Unforgettable • When I Fall in Love • The Wind Beneath My Wings • and more.
02501006 P/V/G...$19.95

Prices, contents, and availability subject to change without notice.

cherry lane
music company
www.cherrylane.com

EXCLUSIVELY DISTRIBUTED BY
HAL•LEONARD® CORPORATION
7777 W. BLUEMOUND RD. P.O. BOX 13819 MILWAUKEE, WI 53213

0610